AF505691

FIGHTING INDIANS IN
WASHINGTON TERRITORY

Erasmus Darwin Keyes

FIGHTING INDIANS

IN

WASHINGTON TERRITORY

BY

GENERAL ERASMAS D. KEYES

YE GALLEON PRESS
FAIRFIELD, WASHINGTON

Library of Congress Cataloging-in-Publication Data

Keyes, Erasmus, D. (Erasmus Darwin), 1810-1895.
  [Fifty years' observation of men and events]
  Fighting Indians in Washington territory — Erasmus D. Keyes.
  p. cm.
  Reprint. Originally published: Fifty years' observation of men and
events. New York: Scribner, 1884.

  1. Keyes, Erasmus D. (Erasmus Darwin), 1810-1895. 2. Pacific
Coast Indians, Wars with 1847-1865. 3. United States — History —
Civil War, 1861-1865 — Personal narratives. 4. Peninsula Campaign,
1862 — Personal narratives. 5. Scott. Winfield, 1786-1866. 6 Pioneers
— Washington (State) — Biography. 7. Washington (State) —
Biography. I. Title.

F891.K47   1988   88-116   979.7'03'0924-dc19
ISBN 0-87770-445-7

INTRODUCTION

Erasmus Darwin Keyes, author of this material on fighting Indians in Oregon and Washington Territories in the 1850's was born on May 29, 1810 in the village of Brimfield, Massachusetts. He was the son of Justus Keyes and Elizabeth (Corey) Keyes. Justus Keyes was a well known physician in Brimfield but later moved to Kennebec County, Maine. Erasmus Keyes obtained an appointment to the West Point Military Academy from which he was commissioned a second lieutenant in the Third Artillery. He was aide-de-camp to General Winfield Scott 1837-1838. On November 30, 1831 he was promoted to the rank of captain in the Third Artillery, was stationed at New Orleans and later at Fort Moultrie, South Carolina. He was then given a post as instructor of field artillery and cavalry at West Point. He returned to active military service and from 1851 to 1860 was stationed at various western posts, including Fort Walla Walla, Washington Territory. From this post he experienced combat with eastern Washington Indians. Following the humiliating defeat of troops under Col. Edward J. Steptoe near present-day Rosalia, Keyes, along with a number of other soldiers and officers, was shipped from San Francisco to Fort Vancouver and up river to Fort Walla Walla where he served under George Wright, commander of the Ninth Infantry, fighting in the Indian battles of Four Lakes and Spokane Plains in the early autumn of 1858. He had earlier, in 1855, some Indian fighting experience in western Washington. On October 12, 1858 he was promoted to major, First Artillery. In 1860 and 1861 he served as military secretary to General Scott with rank of lieutenant-colonel. On May 14, 1861, while the Civil War was still in progress, he resigned from the U.S. Army and moved to San Francisco where he engaged in grape culture and the savings and loan business. On November 8, 1837 Keyes had married Caroline M. Clark, by whom he had five children. His wife died in 1853 and several years later, on November 22, 1862 he married Mary (Loughborough) Bissel, who also had five children. Death came to Erasmus Keyes in Nice, France, while on a European tour with his second wife. He was buried at West Point on November 19, 1895. He is author of a book of Civil War experiences, *Fifty Years' Observation of Men and Events*, from which his experiences fighting Indians in Washington Territory in the 1850's was extracted.

REGARDING the outbreak of the Indians in the
Puget Sound district of Washington Territory,
which occurred in 1855, and the war which followed, I
shall confine my remarks to a limited space. The hostili-
ty of the tribes was so general in all the Territory, and
their devastations so cruel in many places, that General
John E. Wool, who commanded the Department of the
Pacific, thought it requisite to repair in person to Fort
Vancouver. My company, "M," Third Regiment of Artillery, embarked with him on board the steamer California, Captain William E. Dall, and proceeded northward, early in November, 1855. We arrived off the
mouth of the Columbia River in the afternoon,
and although a fierce wind had covered the whole bar
from shore to shore and for several miles up and down
with a white foam, it was decided to cross at once. There
happened to be a pilot on board, and he and the captain
stood together on the bridge. The head of steam was increased to secure steerage-way in the billows, and we
moved up against a strong ebb tide at a fair rate of
speed till we reached about midway in the passage, when
a flue collapsed, drove all the burning coals from under
one of the boilers, and set fire to the ship, which immedi-

ately lost headway so much that she ceased for a moment to obey her rudder. The pilot lost courage, exclaimed, "She's a goner!" and started down from the bridge. Captain Dall instantly resumed command, called out to the firemen to feed the remaining fires with lard and tallow, and after a few seconds the ship began to move forward, and at the end of an hour we were anchored off Astoria.

When the steamer lost headway the lead showed a draught of water almost exactly corresponding with that of the vessel, but fortunately she did not ground. If she had struck, not a soul on board could by possibility have been saved. Some of the soldiers, as they saw the pilot quitting his post, came to me in terror, and asked what they should do. I replied, "Take hold of that hose and let us put out that fire in the hold." I carried the end of the hose down the steps as far as I could breathe, the men pumped, and in a short time the flames were extinguished. General Wool was perfectly calm, as were the other officers, but it is certain none of us ever escaped a greater danger than on that occasion, and such was the opinion of the eight or ten shipmasters who were among the passengers. Captain Dall's intrepidity was the admiration of every man on board the ship.

From the Columbia River, General Wool ordered me to proceed in another transport to Steilacoom and assume command of the Puget Sound District. I arrived there on the 24th day of November, 1855, and found a condition of wild alarm. Many families had been massacred, and the surviving settlers were all collected in the small towns. There were only two skeleton companies of regular infantry and a few companies of volunteers in the district, and they were widely scattered. Lieutenant Slaughter, with one company, guarded a stockade at the north of the Puyallup, and I arranged an interview with him with the aid of a friendly Indian. I went out twenty miles from Fort Steilacoom, and conversed with him across the river, which was so deep and rapid that my volunteer messenger, after delivering my note to Slaughter, lost his horse in returning, but saved himself. Slaughter assured me that he was safe from attack in his strong block-house, with plenty of supplies, and that, owing to the high state of the water in the streams and the smallness of my force in men and animals, it would be folly to invade the Indian country before the arrival of reinforcements, and the subsidence of the streams. Recommending caution and vigilance on his part, I returned to my post.

Four days later, to wit, on the 4th of December, Lieutenant Slaughter was killed by a party of Indians, headed by the famous Klicitat Chief, Kanaskat. As William A. Slaughter was a graduate of the West Point Military Academy of the class of 1848, and a pupil of mine, I will transcribe the circumstances of his death from my journal.

" *December 7*, 1855.—At about 4.30 to-day, news was brought that Lieutenant Slaughter, 4th Infantry, had been shot by the Indians. On the 3d instant he left his camp at Morrison's, near the Puyallup, with fifty-four soldiers. He had with him Lieutenant James E. Harrison of the marine corps, and Dr. Taylor of the navy. On the afternoon of the 4th they arrived at a deserted farm on Brannan's Prairie, which is two miles from the fork of White and Green rivers, where there is a post commanded by Captain Hewett of the volunteers. Hewett came up to see Slaughter, and to tell him he had been scouting over the neighborhood all day, and that he found no signs of Indians. As Slaughter, who had come from another direction, discovered none, they considered themselves safe, and they allowed fires to be built and kept burning long after dark. In this they made a fatal mistake, as among hostile savages there is no safety except by keeping dark and well guarded. This I had learned from my service in Florida, and that in a campaign against Indians, the front is all around, and the rear nowhere.

" The men were busy cooking their suppers, and the officers, Slaughter, Hewett, Harrison, and Taylor, were conversing in a small log hut, which stood near the fence at the edge of the prairie. All this while a band of red skins, directed by Kanaskat, were creeping up and arranging themselves in a thicket of brush and tall grass that stood a hundred yards distant. The sentinel had noticed the rustling of the grass, and heard what he supposed was the grunting of hogs, and as the settlers had often left their animals at their farms, he paid no attention to those noises. At a little past seven o'clock, the Indians fired a volley, aimed mostly at the hut. One bullet passed between the logs and directly through Slaughter's heart. He fell over and expired in a minute. His only words were : ' Take care of yourselves, I am dying !' Two corporals were killed outright, and four private soldiers wounded, one of whom died the following day. After a single volley the Indians withdrew."

Among the Indian chiefs of the Puget Sound district were five whose names were on every tongue. These were Pat Kanim, Kanaskat, Kitsap, Quimelt, and Leschi. Pat Kanim remained friendly, although he confessed to me that he had two tum tums (hearts), one of which inclined him to fight the *Bostons* (whites), and the other to keep the peace because he thought them too strong ! The other four were hostile, and Kanaskat, above the others, was the most deadly foe to our race. This chief was engaged in nearly all the murders that brought on the conflict. He was not only noted for the ingenious devices of torture that he would practise on his victims, but for the ferocious pertinacity with which he began and continued the war. He boasted that he could prolong it five years, and that no bullet could kill him.

Cutmouth John and other messengers who came to me from the hostile camp all gave the same account of Kanaskat. He would have nothing to say about peace, but would sit apart in obstinate sulkiness. Kanaskat's reputation extended beyond the mountains, and Ohwi sent his son Qualchein and another young brave from the Yackima country to learn from him the art of fighting in the night time. He was a model Indian patriot, hardy and enterprising, perfect in feral stealth, and vengeance was his ruling quality. He hated all the white settlers, and rather than they should possess his country he preferred to perish. It chanced that I laid the plan which resulted in the death of Kanaskat, as will appear from the following account which I wrote in my journal the day it occurred.

I transcribe all the facts as then recorded:

Colonel Silas Casey, of the 9th Infantry, having arrived with reinforcements of men and animals, a force under his command left Fort Steilacoom on the 26th of February 1846, to operate against the Indians. We crossed the Puyallup at a point eighteen miles distant to a post commanded by Captain Maurice Malony. Here we remained till the morning of the 28th, and then marched eight miles up the right bank to Lemmon's Prairie, and pitched our tents.

Lemmon's Prairie is small, and at that time it was bordered with a fringe of trees and bushes on the side of the river, from which it is distant about half a mile. On the opposite side was a wooded steep hill, at the base of which was a narrow stream spanned by a bridge of logs. From thence a wood road wound up the hill into the country of the hostiles.

Being second in command, I was detailed officer of the day, and became responsible for the safety of the camp. After guard mounting, I took with me the non-commissioned officers, and with them made the entire circuit of the camp, keeping within and near the fringe of trees and brush all the way around. On the river side I ordered single sentinels to be posted, but on the slope of the hill I found two points from which an enemy might fire upon the tents. At the first I ordered three guards to be posted, of which one sentinel would stand in a spot which I indicated, and the other two would lie down near by. Then proceeding along 150 yards, I came to the trail leading up the hill, and selected another post for three men as at the first. From this the sentinel could look up the road 100 yards to where it made an angle to the left. After that, I continued my circuit to a spot where I obtained a view up the road beyond the elbow. It was in a small open space, near a large tree from the shadow of which an Indian could watch the officers coming out of their tents at break of day, fire on them, and retreat in safety. I therefore ordered Sergeant Newton of my company, who was the chief non-commissioned officer of the guard, to establish the picket here instead of at the crossing of the trail. The sergeant differed so strongly in opinion from me that he ventured to remonstrate, but I over-ruled him, and told him that the place where we stood was decidedly the best of all, and that good men must occupy it. I gave minute directions for the sentinel to stand near the trunk of the tree, and watch the road up the hill above the turn, for if the Indians came they must certainly come that way.

Having completed the circuit of the camp, and made myself acquainted with every possible approach to it, I returned and made another inspection of the guard. Observing that Private Kehl, of Company D, of the 9th Infantry, had a determined countenance, I selected him for one of the important picket guards. Then I addressed the men as follows: (I will copy here the exact words of my journal) "You must take care to-night not to make a false alarm. I am the officer of the day, and should consider myself disgraced by a false alarm. Be sure that you fire at nothing but an Indian, and be sure also if you do fire that you get him."

Private Kehl, with his two companions, went to the post assigned them, and in the morning, soon after five o'clock, Kehl was standing sentinel under the tree. It was before daybreak, but the cooks had already lighted their fires, and the watchful soldier saw a gleam of light reflected from the barrel of a rifle a hundred yards up the trail beyond the bend. Then in a few minutes he saw five Indians in single file creeping stealthily down the hill. The one in front was waving his right hand backward to caution the four who followed him. Kehl stood motionless till the leader came nearly abreast of him; then with deliberate aim he fired, and the great chief Kanaskat fell. At the report of his shot, I ran out to the bridge, where I heard Sergeant Newton forty yards beyond cry out, "We've got an Indian!" He and another man were dragging him along by the heels. The savage had been shot through the spine, and his legs were paralyzed, but the strength of his arms and voice was not affected. He made motions to draw a knife. I ordered two soldiers to hold him, and it required all their strength to do so. As they dragged him across the bridge, I followed, and he continued to call out in a language I did not understand. Some one came up who recognized the wounded Indian, and exclaimed, " Kanaskat !" "Nawitka !" said he with tremendous energy, his voice rising to a scream—" Kanaskat—Tyee—Mamelouse nica—nica mamelouse *Bostons* "—*yes, Kanaskat—chief—Kill me, I kill Bostons.* He added, " My heart is wicked towards the whites, and always will be, and you had better kill me." Then he began to call out in his native language, not a word of which could any of us understand. I ordered two soldiers to stop his mouth, but they were unable to do so. He appeared to be yelling for his comrades, and two other shots were fired from the pickets on the hill, when Corporal O'Shaughnessy, who was standing by, placed the muzzle of his rifle close to the chieftain's temple, blew a hole through his head, and scattered the brains about.

During all the frantic imprecations of the prostrate savage, I was standing only two yards from his feet, looking at his face. I have seen men in rage, and women in despair, and maniacs, but never before did I gaze on a human countenance in which hate and blasted hope were so horribly depicted, as in that of Kanaskat. It seemed to me, while I was regarding the fierce contortions and burning gaze of the dying chief, that I was in the presence of a defiant demon whose fitting habitation was the most algent cavern of Hell.

After death the countenance of Kanaskat wore the expression natural to it in life, saving that the infernal fires that glowed from the depth of his eyeballs had gone out with the vital spark. There was a diabolical fascination in the massive jaw, fixed scowl, and bronzed skin of the monster's visage, that drew me to cross the field several times to gaze on it where he lay, face up and eyes wide open. I even dismounted from my horse, when ready to march, and wandered apart to look on him once more. It seemed that every moment of his life had deposited a particle of matter to form a perfect image of vengeance. There was no line that pity or tenderness, or holy meditation had ever traced upon it. It presented a scene of absolute moral desolation more awful than the Dead Sea or the crater of Etna.

Regarding the carcass of the dead chief as that of an unclean animal that men hunt for the love of havoc, we left it in the field unburied, and went on our way to fight his people.

Leaving Lemmon's Prairie on the morning of March 1, we advanced into the enemy's country, and at mid-day we were met by two messengers, a white man and an Indian, sent by Lieutenant A. V. Kautz of the 9th Infantry, to inform us that he, with his company, was held at bay on the right bank of White River by a large body of Indians. Kautz's men were intrenched within a huge pile of dead timber and trees that had collected on the edge of the stream. Colonel Casey immediately detached me with fifty-four soldiers to go to his relief. I took the Indian boy, who was only fifteen years old, for guide. We pushed forward with all possible speed a distance of eight or nine miles, but instead of leading me to the ford, the young rascal conducted us to a point half a mile below, where the contracted torrent was absolutely impassable. I called the boy to me and told him to show me the crossing, or I would shoot him on the spot. He replied, "*Nica cumtux*" (I know), and led the way through the woods to a place where the river spread out to three times its width below. I ordered the soldiers to fasten their cartridge-boxes about their shoulders, and then we dashed in and passed over without accident, although the water, which was ice-cold, came up to the armpits of the short men, and ran like a mill-race.

Between the water's edge and the bluff on the opposite side of the river was a grass-covered slope about two hundred yards wide. The bluff or bank was not high, and it was so thickly covered with trees and brush that not an enemy could be seen. I deployed my men as skirmishers, and Kautz, who had left the wood-pile, did the same, and I ordered the whole to charge. The Indians fired a volley, enough to kill every one of us, but they aimed too high, and only one man was struck, and that was Lieutenant Kautz. A rifle-ball passed through his leg, but I was not aware that he had been wounded until the battle was over. After one discharge, the Indians ran, and we pursued them through the woods half a mile, at double quick time, to the base of a steep hill, on the brow of which they made a stand, and, with derisive epithets, dared us to come on. The slope of the hill for a distance of 200 yards was bare, and at the top were many large standing and fallen trees, which afforded cover to the enemy and gave him a great advantage. Lieutenant David B. McKibbin of Kautz's Company, 9th Infantry, was in line with the front rank, and when half way up the slope the savages arose with a whoop and opened fire. Several soldiers fell, but McKibbin's gallantry encouraged the others, and not one flinched. I was at the moment just coming up the slope of the hill, and we all pressed forward, and in a short time our victory was complete. Our number engaged was 100, and we lost two killed and eight wounded. The smallness of our loss was probably due to the bravery of the men, who rushed upon the Indians, disconcerting them, and fifty of their shots went over our heads for every one that took effect.

The death of their most warlike chief, and the decisive victory we achieved on the first of March, dismayed the redskins, and thereafter all their energies were exerted to avoid a battle with the regulars, although they fought afterwards with the volunteers. We hunted and pursued them almost without intermission night or day for two months, over hills and dales, through swamps and thickets. It rained more than half the time, and the influence of Mount Regnier and its vast, eternal covering of snow upon the temperature made the nights excessively cold. Such was our liability to surprise, that we were obliged to be ready to fight at all times, and there was not an hour of darkness during the active operations that I could not have stood outside my tent equipped at the end of one minute from the first sound of alarm. The hardships of that campaign, in which the pluck and endurance of Kautz, Sukely, Mendell, and several others were so severely tested, caused me afterwards to regard the seven days' fight before Richmond as a comparative recreation. I was the second in rank to Colonel Silas Casey, who had had much experience on the frontiers. My position was one which, in the army, frequently provokes grumbling and censoriousness, but I found no fault with his arrangements, and thought he displayed decided ability in the conduct of his campaign. A year later I had a conversation in San Francisco with Colonel Casey as he was embarking for Washington. He then stated to me that the victory of March 1st, 1856, in which I commanded, saved the Government not less than $5,000,000. He also said on the same occasion that the plan I laid resulted in the killing of the Chief Kanaskat. He promised to use his influence to have me breveted, and he expected a brevet for himself, which he certainly deserved. In those days, however, when Mr. Jefferson Davis was

Secretary of War, the exploits of Northern officers were not much regarded, and neither of us received the slightest notice.

In my plan to kill Kanaskat I suspended two regulations—one that required a single sentinel to *walk* his post, and thus to enable a skulking savage to see and avoid him, and another which prescribed the relief of the sentinels at intervals of one or two hours by a detachment of the guard making its rounds for that purpose or to see if they are awake. I posted three men in a single spot where they were all concealed under trees and behind logs or stones, with orders for one to stand still and watch, and from time to time to awaken the man who was to take his place.

The above-described plan originated with me, so far as I know. Its originality with me is conceded by General A. V. Kautz, of the United States Infantry, and Colonel George H. Mendell, of the Engineer Corps, both of whom were most efficient actors with me in the campaign of 1856, and are men of unimpeachable integrity. After writing my account of our operations, I received letters from those two officers corroborative of my descriptions.

Surgeon George Sukeley, whom I have already mentioned, was with us on nearly all our scouting expeditions. He was a man of genius and devoted to science. His activity of body and mind was extraordinary, and he was equally admired by the army, the citizens, and the friendly Indians. He collected and forwarded to the Smithsonian Institute a vast number of beasts, birds, fishes, reptiles, and insects peculiar to the country we were in; likewise many bones, jaws, and skulls of dead Indians. He also sent the head of an enormous wolf, which one of the sentinels shot while on post at Muckleshoot Prairie. He had in his employ an old squaw who was able to tell him the Indian names of every quadruped, snake, worm, bug, insect, fish, creeping, swimming, flying, or burrowing animal that he found, and many that he did not find, but which she discovered and brought to him. If Cuvier or Agassiz had known of the existence of that squaw they would have gone half round the world to consult her, for she was an unexampled genius and a veritable she Aristotle.

We had another gentleman, Mr. George Gibbs, who was in civil government employ and who was a member of the officers' mess at Steilacoom, and who is worthy of mention for the reason that he possessed many accomplishments and amiable qualities. Gibbs devoted much time to the dialects of the aborigines, and became a master of the Chinook jargon. All unwritten languages are difficult to learn, but he was able to speak them so well that he astonished the Indians themselves. The Chinook dialect is made up of the distorted and truncated words and phrases of the Russian, English, French, and native languages. It was remarked that Gibbs could speak Chinook better than any other man, white or red. He came down to San Francisco, and one morning put on the dress and headgear which he had worn among the savages. In that rig he entered a fashionable shop to make purchases. He inquired for various articles, but none of the shopmen could comprehend him. They sent out for linguists of various nations and tribes, of which there were many in the city, but not one could speak Chinook. Gibbs wore a long beard and a serious countenance, and appeared anxious to make himself understood. Finally, after babbling his jargon for half an hour, he walked away, leaving the wondering crowd to conjecture his nationality.

The Indian war in the Puget Sound district being at an end, I was ordered by Colonel Casey in the month of October, 1856, to return to my post, the delightful Presidio of San Francisco. The year succeeding was too barren of incident to require especial notice.

In the month of May, 1858, I was a member of a court-martial convened at Fort Miller, on the San Joaquin River. Captain E. O. C. Ord was the commanding officer, and his family were with him at his post. They entertained the members of the court-martial bountifully, and the loving harmony of that household was delightful to observe. Ord was cheerful and domestic in his habits, and his accomplished wife told me that her life had been joyous. Little did she foresee what the future had in store for her gallant husband, or what sorrow for herself. General Ord, although a Virginian by birth, illustrated his name in the Northern armies during our civil war. If we except General Crook, for a shorter time he probably did as much constant hard service as any other officer in the army. After forty years of active duty he was retired, went to Mexico, where he exercised important civil functions, and married one of his daughters to a general of that country. Being still in vigorous health and prosperous, he left Vera Cruz in the month of August, 1883, for a trip to Cuba, and while on board the ship was taken down with yellow fever and died.

It was on the very site of Fort Miller, in the same month of May seven years before, that I saw assembled above 1,200 aborigines, natives of the adjacent plains and mountains, many of whom had never seen a white man till they came to treat with us. I was then impressed with the appearance of several chiefs, and remembered the general aspect of all. Especially was I struck with the activity of the young Indians of both sexes while they amused themselves with football and other rough sports. As all those Indians had been assigned to a reservation of which Fort Miller was a central point, I inquired for several individuals whom I remembered. I was told that they were nearly all dead, victims to drunkenness, and that of the whole number I then saw in such full activity not above fifty remained. I took pains to see the wretched survivors, and was shocked with the spectacle of degradation and self-abandonment they presented.

To show the care bestowed upon its copper-colored wards by our Government when it collected them upon reservations, I might relate many incidents that I have learned by observation and credible report, but shall limit myself to one. The commissioners, McKee, Woozencroft, and Barbour, made generous provisions for the denizens of the San Joaquin Valley. The reservations were extensive, and the Indians were to be supplied with agricultural implements, seeds, work animals, blacksmiths, schools, and many other useful things, the most essential to them being beef cattle. About ten years subsequent to the treaties made by those commissioners, a herdsman who had been employed by contractors to furnish beeves to these Indians on their reservations declared to me, as a solemn truth, that he had delivered and had receipted for one and the same old Toruno (stag) twenty-seven times. The weight of that beast was entered in the accounts and paid for at figures varying from 1,000 to 1,100 pounds. That old stag was an energetic quadruped, and would break loose invariably the night after he was receipted for, and return to the corral to which he was habituated, and where he was always well cared for. If I were to write a treatise on the relations between theoretic and practical benevolence, I should select for my subject the Indian policy of the United States Government.

Towards the end of May, 1858, news was received in San Francisco of Colonel Steptoe's disaster at the north of Snake River, Washington Territory. The Colonel had been detached from Walla Walla with 159 men to capture cattle thieves, and while on his march towards Fort Colville he was attacked by a thousand or more Spokans, Pelouses, Cœur d'Alenes, and Yackimas, and obliged to retreat. His small band defended themselves from morning till night, and Captain H. P. Taylor, Lieutenant William Gaston, and several of the rank and file were killed. The balance had the good fortune to get away in the darkness, and at ten o'clock on the morning of the 17th, after a ride of 75 miles, they reached a place of safety at the south of the river. Considering the fatigue of a whole day's fighting with the Indians, the flight of 75 miles during the succeeding night, without the loss of a man that started, was an evidence of endurance that has few examples in history.

General N. S. Clark, the commander of the Department of the Pacific, lost no time in sending northward all the available troops in California. I arrived at the Dalles with two companies on the 21st of June, and on the 24th was joined by two other companies, the four being under my orders and all encamped together. From the 25th of June till the 7th of July I lost no time in preparing my force to fight the Indians. I had numerous targets the height of a man set up at various distances on even and uneven ground, and for several hours every day, Sundays not excepted, I caused the soldiers, individually and collectively, to fire at those targets. In every case they were required to estimate the distance, which was afterwards told, and required to adjust their aim accordingly. The effect of that drilling was wonderful, and I estimated it as giving a quadruple value to my numbers. I told the men that our operations would probably be in an open prairie country, and that their muskets being of a longer range than those sold by the Hudson Bay Company to the enemy, they could aim at an Indian as securely as at a plank.

The march of 177 miles from the Dalles to Walla Walla was fatiguing, as the weather was excessively hot, and in places the ground was so difficult that it occupied twelve days. Colonel George H. Wright of the Ninth Infantry was assigned to the command of the expedition, and it required time to organize and send forward his little army to the point on the south side of the Snake River which he selected to cross to the country of the hostiles. It was at the mouth of a little stream called the Tucanon, and in obedience to orders, as soon as I arrived there in the advance I caused a small fort to be constructed, which was left in charge of Brevet Major F. O. Wyse, with one company of artillery.

I had never before served under the orders of Colonel Wright, but from a slight personal acquaintance with him and many favorable reports I had conceived great respect for his military capacity. I was glad, therefore, to be his lieutenant, and to receive from him the command of a battalion of six companies of artillery serving as infantry. Major William N. Grier commanded the dragoons, about 200 in number; Lieutenant White, the mountain howitzer company; Captain Winder, a company of riflemen, and Lieutenant Dent, brother-in-law to General Grant, a company of infantry. Lieutenant John Mullan had under his orders 33 friendly Nez Perces Indians, who were to act as guides, scouts, and interpreters. Mullan was also the topographical engineer of the expedition, and he was well acquainted with the country we were to operate in. Captain R. W. Kirkham was quartermaster and commissary. Surgeon J. F. Hammond, brother to Senator Hammond of South Carolina and author of the expression "mudsills," was the chief of the medical staff, Lieutenant P. A. Owen acting adjutant-general, and Lieutenant L. Kipp, Third Artillery, adjutant of my battalion.

All the detachments, numbering about 900 men, having arrived, we crossed the river on the 25th and 26th days of August—the men, baggage, provisions for 40 days, and ammunition in boats, of which there was a great scarcity, and about 700 mules and horses swimming the rapid stream, with Indians alongside the leaders to keep them headed towards the opposite shore. That was a singular and amusing sight. It was a stupendous task to pack 400 mules the next morning, but Kirkham's arrangements were so effective that it was accomplished at five o'clock, at which hour we left the river to find the enemy.

Numerous reports and stories had reached us that the Indians were exulting in their victory over Steptoe, and they were confident that not a man of us who crossed the Snake River would return alive. On the 30th of August they first showed themselves in small scouting parties, and the next day they appeared in considerable numbers, skirting our line of march for several hours, but keeping out of gunshot. They were apparently luring us on to a favorable spot they had previously selected to attack and destroy us.

Towards the end of our march, on the 31st of August, Colonel Wright and his escort having preceded me about half a mile and encamped, the Indians set fire to the grass, and under cover of the smoke, approached and fired upon the rear guard. We had kept the pack train well closed, and upon hearing the first shots I ordered the three companies of Winder, Ihrie, and Hardie and Dent to deploy at double-quick time as skirmishers across the rear and along the two sides of the column, while the front was well protected by Captain Ord. Within five minutes from the first command the whole train and everything else was enclosed in a rectangle of armed men, and the attack repulsed. The promptness of the manœuvre was admirable, and showed the benefit of discipline and previous instruction.

The battle of the Four Lakes was fought on the 1st of September, 1858. It was not Colonel Wright's intention to attack that day, but to rest the men and animals in the beautiful camp established the evening before. His determination was changed, however, by the appearance in the morning of a considerable body of the enemy on a neighboring hill, and the report of our Nez Perces scouts of many more beyond. The Colonel having arranged his plan, the whole force, with the exception of a guard to protect the camp and pack-train, marched about a mile to the foot of the eminence, from whence Gregg's dragoons, Ord's company, and Mullan with his scouts were ordered up to dislodge the hostiles, which was quickly done. Then our commander ascended with his staff, followed by me and my battalion and the artillery. When we reached the summit we halted a few minutes to view an animated spectacle. We could see the four lakes and the gullies and patches of woods bordering the water, and a vast plain stretching away to the front and left. The natural scenery was interesting, but its effect was wonderfully heightened by the thousand or more savage warriors who were riding furiously hither and thither over the plain or issuing from the woods and valleys. The barbarous host was armed with Hudson Bay muskets, spears, bows and arrows, and apparently they were subject to no order or command. The brilliant morning sun, which illuminated the purest air of the continent, enabled me to distinguish through my field-glass the individual savages, their horses, their trappings, and equipments. Both men and animals were smeared and striped with gaudy pigments and bedecked with the feathers and plumes of birds of prey. The skins of bears, wolves, and the buffalo served generally for saddles, and the whole display was enhanced by the frantic gestures and yells of the warriors, who brandished their weapons in defiance.

Colonel Wright indicated to me my point of attack, and I descended to the plain, where I ordered several companies to deploy as skirmishers and to advance firing. Our first discharge seemed to surprise the Indians, and those nearest scampered off, but some would turn back and fire upon us. After clearing the broken ground, we made way for Grier to pass on the right. He ordered his men to charge, and they started off handsomely, but his horses had been marching without a day's rest for nearly a month, and they scarcely gained on the hardy Indian ponies, which were all fresh. Lieutenant Gregg, who was a splendid *sabreur*, overtook one of the flying rascals, and with a blow of his blade split his skull in two. I pursued and fought the enemy nearly three hours, and upon reaching a hill over which the savages had disappeared I was obliged to halt the advance to allow a considerable number of the soldiers who were fatigued and overheated to come up. On reaching the crest of the hill I could see not more than ten or fifteen Indians, the main body having fled to the woods beyond. While I was halted the recall was sounded, and I returned to camp after an absence of about four hours. The plain was scattered with Indian muskets, bows, arrows, blankets, skins and trinkets which had been abandoned by the warriors in their flight, but they had carried off their killed and wounded, according to custom. We could not ascertain from observation during the fight the exact loss of the enemy, but we were certain that a considerable number were slain, and from subsequent enquiry and information, we concluded that not less than sixty Indians were killed and wounded. Of my battalion not a man was hit. As I had anticipated, our long-ranged arms, discipline, and careful previous instruction secured our safety, and enabled us to thin the number of the savages until their panic-flight took them beyond our reach. The importance of the victory of the Four Lakes was not the less for having been bloodless for us, and it stimulated the soldiers greatly.

The men and animals needed rest; we remained in camp at the Four Lakes until six o'clock on the morning of September 5, when we resumed our advance. At first we saw no Indians, but at the end of an hour they began to show themselves, and to move along parallel with our line of march over the rough ground, beyond which was the great Spokan Plain. We had advanced far within the prairie, when, all at once, we saw the savages setting fire to the tall dry grass with which the plain was covered nearly all around us. A strong wind was blowing in our faces, and the flames were shooting high and constantly extending. Our situation was sufficiently alarming when we discovered, a few hundred yards to the front and left, a patch of bare rock and scant herbage. Upon that we collected our animals in haste, and the drivers put out the fire on the short stubble, which gave room and saved us from a stampede. Meanwhile the enemy had opened fire upon us, and our men passed through where the flames were least, Grier and his dragoons leading, and commenced the *battle of Spokan Plains*. That battle ended fourteen miles from where it began, and the field upon which it was fought embraced hills and ravines, woods, rocks, and bare level ground. I kept one, and occasionally two, companies in close order, and the others deployed, so that my line of battle was often above a mile long. The woods and openings alternated in long strips, and riding at full speed to and fro, along the rear, enabled me to see the Indians when they passed across those openings, as they did frequently in both directions. As soon as I saw them making to the right or the left, I ordered forward reinforcements to meet them wherever they opened fire. The activity and spirit displayed by the officers of my battalion left nothing to be desired. They certainly did their best and did well. It is not easy to discriminate, and I name them as they occur to my memory—Captains E. O. C. Ord and J. A. Hardie, Lieutenants H. G. Gibson, R. P. Tyler, J. L. White, G. F. B. Dandy, M. R. Morgan, Ihrie, D. R. Ransom, and my adjutant, Lawrence Kipp. There were probably 1,000 Indian warriors opposed to us, and among them were some of the Pend d'Oreilles and the famous Yackima chief, Kammiakin. He was severely wounded by a splinter torn from a tree that was struck by one of White's howitzer shells. On our side not a man was killed, and only one wounded. The loss of the enemy was considerable, but it could not be ascertained, on account of their invariable habit of carrying away their killed and wounded. The country fought over was without water, and when we reached the Spokan River, and pitched our camp, twenty-five miles distant from the former, the whole command, men and animals, were nearly exhausted. It was estimated that I had ridden eighty miles on the same pony of incredible endurance. I kept my saddle till my tent was pitched; then I dismounted, took a glass of wine, gave orders not to disturb me, and lay down on my back to rest. For half an hour I did not move a muscle, and felt the whole time that if I did move one I should die. At the end of an hour I was restored, and no one had noticed my debility. Never before, or since, was I so nearly finished by the toil of war.

September 8.—Instead of crossing the Spokan River we kept up along the south bank over an extensive grassy plain. As we advanced we saw a great cloud of dust rising up far ahead. Then we discovered what we mistook for a patch of brown, bare earth on the side of the mountain, but by close watching we saw it move. It was a band of cattle. After marching eight miles further, the train was halted and left in charge of Ord's and Gibson's companies of artillery and a company of dragoons. Gregg's, with the balance of my command, I pushed forward, following Colonel Wright and staff, Grier's three companies of dragoons, and the Nez Perces guides. I marched my foot-soldiers eighteen miles at quick time, without a halt, to the top of a range of hills. From their summit we discovered, far across a beautiful lake and plain, many moving specks, which were horses. Grier had overtaken and captured them without opposition. The band consisted of about 1,000 horses, mares, and colts, which were the property of a *Tyee* whose name was Tilcohitz; and he was a great thief and rascal.

At first Colonel Wright and others were not disposed to kill the horses, thinking them too valuable. I told him I should not sleep so long as they remained alive, as I regarded them the main dependence and most prized of all the possessions of the Indians, who would find a way to stampede them. Finally the Colonel organized a board of officers, of which I was president, to determine what should be done with the horses. The board decided to allow the officers and the quartermaster to select a certain number, and the friendly Indians were to choose one or two each, and in this way about 20 were disposed of for the present. For the others a high enclosure was constructed, the poor animals driven in, and the work of shooting commenced. The soldiers soon learned that by planting a bullet just behind the ears the animal would drop dead at once. In two days the number shot by actual tally was 690, and the expenditure of cartridges about twice as many. It was a cruel sight to see so many noble beasts shot down. They were all sleek, glossy, and fat, and as I love a horse, I fancied I saw in their beautiful faces an appeal for mercy. Towards the last the soldiers appeared to exult in their bloody task; and such is the ferocious character of men.

While the work of destruction was going on I saw an Indian approaching our camp, carrying in his hand a long pole from which a strip of white cloth was flying, and in the cleft end of the pole was a letter. The letter was from Father Joset, S. J., of the Cœur d'Alene mission, written to inform Colonel Wright that in consequence of our victories the hostiles were completely cast down, and that they wished him to be their intercessor for peace. The father added in his communication that the friendlies were delighted at our victories, as they had been threatened with punishment by the hostiles for not fighting.

On the 11th of September we crossed the Spokan, and ours was the first civilized army that ever passed that stream. Our first march beyond was through a rich agricultural country, where we found many rude huts and numerous stacks of wheat. The dragoons all fed their horses with wheat, and each carried away one or two sheaves. The large balance we burned, so that desolation marked our tracks. We encamped on the edge of the beautiful Cœur d'Alene Lake, and after a tedious march over a narrow trail through the mountain forest we arrived, on the 13th, at the mission of the same name.

The next day I visited the mission, which was established in 1846. The church was built of logs, spacious, but unfinished. Everything within and around had a rustic appearance. Father Joset, Father Minitree, and two lay brothers were there. In this savage, out-of-the-way place they were obliged to live and labor with the aborigines. In the evening I supped with the fathers. They had plenty of excellent beef, vegetables, and milk, but the table and its service were as plain as possible.

In Father Joset I found a cultivated gentleman in the prime of life, fit to adorn the most polished society in the world. I was unable to restrain my expressions of astonishment when he informed me that he had passed the last fourteen years in the wilderness with the savages. I asked him if he had no longings for a better life and society. "No," said he, "I am content and happy where I am. In your profession an outward obedience to orders is all that is required of you, but in the society to which I belong obedience must be internal, and cheerful, and ready. I am happy, and have no desire to exchange situations with any person."

Twice every day while I remained at the mission I had conversations with Father Joset, which increased my admiration for his character and my estimation of his self-denial. He instructed me how his Church had preserved the traditions and dogmas of Christianity, and sustained the purity of the faith, and it was primarily due to his influence that I enrolled myself, at a subsequent date, in the Roman Catholic Church. By his explanations and revelations Father Joset revealed to my mind vistas through which the light from Calvary shone more pure and brilliant than ever before.

The hostiles, who, in the beginning were so confident and audacious, finding themselves absolutely powerless to resist us in the field, changed their policy and became the most humble supplicants for peace. Large numbers came to the mission every day, and on the 17th of September a council was held at which ninety-five chiefs and head men were present, besides numerous squaws and pappooses. The terms of the treaty were not harsh, and old chief Polotkin was so much pleased that he assured Colonel Wright that all his people would cheerfully submit, which they subsequently did.

Vincent, the principal chief of the Cœur d'Alenes, and Polotkin, the head of the Pelouses, both signed the treaty and kept their promises.

While at the mission Colonel Wright invited me to read all his letters, orders and reports. His orders I knew, as they had all been published to the command. I made a careful examination of every document written by the colonel during the campaign, and found in them continual proofs of justice, impartiality, and the absence of prejudice. It seemed to afford him especial satisfaction to set forth the merits of his subordinates, and he omitted no subject worthy of praise, saving his own activity and fitness for command.

All fears of further collisions being at an end, we left the Cœur d'Alene Mission September 18, on our return march. To avoid the narrow trail through the forest, we crossed the Cœur d'Alene River below the lake and also the St. Joseph's. In crossing those deep, clear streams we had the assistance of many Indians with their birch-bark canoes. The white birch grows to an immense size in that northern country—sometimes four feet in diameter and a hundred feet high. The bark is tough, and peels off without breaking, so that a canoe can be made of a single strip. An angular piece is cut out of each end of the sheet of bark, which is brought up, sewed together at the extremes, and the seams smeared with pitch. In that way a boat is made in a short time, but as they are round on the bottom, and without a keel, they are easily capsized.

On the 22d of September we arrived and pitched our camp on the banks of the Nedwall, a small stream, tributary to the Spokan River. Here a treaty was made and signed by chiefs of the Spokans, Calespools and Pelouses. The treaties, among other things, required the surrender of Indian murderers and thieves, and several, eight I think, were surrendered and hanged in this camp. One day six were hanged in two batches. The following is a copy of one of Colonel Wright's laconic orders:

"The three Indians confined last will be executed within an hour.

"Signed, G. WRIGHT,
"Colonel 9th Infantry Com'ing."

It was my habit during the campaign to record the dates of all important movements and transactions, and occasionally I wrote descriptions of events and men in my journal. What follows herein was written in great part directly after the facts occurred:

"In the afternoon of September 22, near night, I observed an old man of medium stature and robust frame, dressed like an American, approaching our camp on horseback. The old man's name was Owhi, brother-in-law to the famous Yackima chief Kammiakin, and father of a young brave named Qualchein, and he came in to make peace, as he said. Old Owhi has a mild expression of countenance, which is assumed, since he has proved himself a double-faced man. He deceived Colonel Wright in his Yackima campaign of 1856, by promising to bring in all his people, and by failing to do so, or to try to do so. After telling Owhi to send for his son Qualchein, he directed the guard to confine the aged chief in irons. At this order the old man's countenance fell completely. He wiped the big drops of sweat from his forehead, dropped his hat, took out his prayer-book, and began to turn the leaves. His skin assumed an ashy pallor, he trembled, and altogether his appearance indicated the profoundest grief and despair.

"September 24.—At about 12 o'clock to-day, as I was standing in front of Colonel Wright's tent, I saw issuing out of a cañon about two hundred yards from me two Indian braves and a handsome squaw. The three rode abreast, and following close behind rode a little hunchback whom I had before seen in our camps. The three principal personages were all gayly dressed, and presented a most dashing air. They all had on a great deal of scarlet, and the squaw sported two ornamental scarfs, passing from the right shoulder under the left arm. She also carried, resting across, in front of her saddle, a long spear, the staff of which was completely wound with various colored beads, and from the ends of which hung two long round pendants of beaver skins. The two braves carried rifles, and one of them had an ornamented tomahawk. I pulled aside the flap of the tent, remarking, as I did so: 'Colonel, we have distinguished strangers here.'" The colonel came out, and after a few minutes' conversation recognized Qualchein, who is the son of Owhi, and one of the most desperate murderers and villains on this coast. He had not met the messenger sent out for him, but came in of his own accord, or perhaps he had been induced to come by the reports of the imp of a hunchback, who looked happy when his party entered our camp.

Having dismounted, Qualchein stood leaning on his rifle talking with Colonel Wright, who stood in front of him, while I was on the right and a few paces in the rear. His bold appearance induced me to watch him closely. The colonel mentioned Owhi's name, at which Qualchein started suddenly and exclaimed, "Car?" (where). Colonel Wright answered calmly, "Owhi mittite yawa" (Owhi is over there). A section of the guard came up, and Qualchein, seeing the hopelessness of his situation, drooped instantly. His eyes watered, and he appeared stupefied, while he repeated several times the words, "*Owhi mittite yawa.*" He was ordered to go with the guard, but he stood still, apparently lost in revery. The soldiers pushed him along to the guard tent and ironed him heavily. Within one hour from his entry into our camp he was hanged by order of Colonel Wright.

Qualchein was a scion of a line of chieftains; his complexion was not so dark as that of the vulgar Indian, and he was a perfect mould of form. His chest was broad and deep, and his extremities small and well shaped. He had the strength of a Hercules, and it required six men to tie his hands and feet, so violent were his struggles, notwithstanding he had an unhealed wound in his side.

In all the battles and forays in Washington Territory, Qualchein was one of the leading spirits, and owing to his youth and hatred of the whites, and his bloody deeds, his influence was probably greater than that of his father, and equal to that of his uncle, the famous Kammiakin. In the action of March 1, 1856, in which I commanded, on White River, Puget Sound district, Qualchein was present with fifty Yackima warriors, of whom he lost seven. He went over the mountains, as he said, "to learn to fight at night." During his life he enjoyed the reputation of bravery and enterprise, but at last, when the rope was around his neck, he begged for mercy in tones that were abject. He promised Captain Dent, who was charged with his execution, horses and *icters* (things) of all kinds, if he would spare his life. Many persons who witnessed his conduct charged him with cowardice and poltroonery, but for myself I took a different view of it. As soon as his hands and feet were bound and the preparations for his death concluded, resistance was out of the question, and love of life was the sole motive of his conduct. He was still young, not over twenty-five years of age, and his physical constitution was apparently perfect —that, and his renown as a prince and warrior, gave to his life a charm and value which he was unwilling to surrender.

On the 26th of September we left the spot, which I called the Camp of Death, on the Nedwall or Lato, and on the 1st day of October we crossed the Snake River on our return. The weather had been, during the last few days of September, cold, rainy, and excessively trying to us all, with our scant supply of clothing. Forewarned of our approach, Major Wyse had ready for all the officers a supper, which we devoured with ravenous appetites. The improvised table groaned under the weight of bunch-grass fed beef (the best in the world), prairie chickens and vegetables. The men were also well supplied with the same good cheer. For us, the major had the foresight to have on hand a basket of champagne, which disappeared down our thirsty throats like water in the sand.

I am now going to transcribe a leaf from my journal

which relates to the aged Yackima chief, Owhi, his power of dissimulation, and his death.

At the advent in Eden of our first parents, Satan in the guise of an angelic page having deceived Uriel, the regent of the sun, and learned from him the way to earth, flew thither, and alighted without the garden. Then at one immense leap, overleaping all bounds, he dropped sheer within, and, like a cormorant, perched upon a tree— thence he proceeded to corrupt our mother Eve. Ever since, and from that time, hypocrites have been numerous among all nations, clans and tribes of men.

"False face must hide what the false heart doth know."

Before setting out on the march of October 3, I committed Owhi, the Indian prisoner, to the charge of Lieutenant M. R. Morgan and his guard of foot-soldiers. The old man appeared reconciled to his fate, and on several occasions he expressed satisfaction at being secure in our protection. We kept him under strict watch, otherwise we treated him with kindness. I often visited him, and it interested me to mark the effects of time (he was seventy years old), bereavement and captivity upon a savage prince, who, in his prime, must have possessed extraordinary physical and mental vigor. I never saw him smile, and frequently deep sadness would mantle his countenance and impart to it an air of dignity. Without doubt he felt sharp pangs, for he had lost all his power, had witnessed the ignominious death of his son, who excelled all his tribe in strength and savage prowess, and now, bereft of hope, he seemed resigned to whatever might be in store for him.

He was mounted upon his own horse, and we had taken the precaution to secure him by a chain and strap attached to his ankles and passing under the saddle-girth.

In this way he rode in silence at the side of Lieutenant Morgan till they came to a rivulet that is a branch of the Tucanon. At the crossing, the stream spread out to the width of seventy-five yards, and about an equal distance above a log spanned it to serve as bridge for footmen. While the soldiers proceeded to pass on the log, Morgan led the Indian's horse across the ford, and dropped the reins when he reached the opposite bank. At the same instant Owhi struck his own horse with violence and made off. Morgan drew his pistol and pursued, firing as he rode. One ball took effect upon the fugitive's horse, which slackened his pace, and enabled the lieutenant to come up abreast. Then, quick as thought, the old man struck Morgan's horse on the head with his whip handle, the size of a wagon spoke, and gave a rough blow with the lash upon the rider's face. At this moment several dragoons approached, and commenced to fire upon Owhi, who was quickly riddled with balls and brought to earth.

When the firing commenced I was a third of a mile away, and suspecting the cause, I rode rapidly in its direction, and met the cavalrymen bringing the dying chief on his own horse, lying across like the carcass of a dead wolf, while his brains were oozing from the bullet-holes in his head.

Surgeon Hammond ordered the old man to be stripped. Two shots had passed through his leg, one into his breast, and one had penetrated under his right cheek-bone, and diagonally up and out near the top of his head, and had destroyed consciousness. The dying chief looked like a gasping bull-dog, and I stood by to see his broad chest heave. He lingered two hours and then expired.

The death scene of this aged Yackima chief presented a strange contrast to that of the Clicitat Tyee, Kanaskat, whose last moments I have already described. The countenance of old Owhi in his last hours was gloomy, not terrible ; but when I recall to mind the dying struggle of Kanaskat I still recoil with horror, after the lapse of seven and twenty years, for I fancied that devils were glaring at me through his eyes, and that his voice was a blast from hell.

On the 5th of October, 1858, we arrived at Walla Walla, and our campaign was at an end. Inspector-General Mansfield being there, after a searching examination, found occasion to compliment us generally. Notwithstanding our long march, the men presented a healthy appearance, which was due in a great measure to the fact that they had lived without whiskey during the last two months or more.

While at Walla Walla we enjoyed the hospitality of the officers stationed there, Steptoe, Dent, and others, and one day there was a feast spread in a large hospital tent, to which several of the Nez Perces chiefs, our allies, were invited. Chief M ses appeared with a sword and scarlet sash and an artillery colonel's dress-coat with large gold epaulettes. Whiskey having been plentifully served, he became brave and loquacious for a time, and then he relapsed, and finally became stupefied, and sank in silence upon his bench, half lying on the table. The feast being over I went away, but an hour later I returned by the tent, and saw old Moses stretched flat on the floor, his feet in the shade, his face in the sun, dead drunk, and asleep.

I doubt if in the history of our country there has ever been an Indian campaign in which so much was accomplished at an equal cost. The good result was due to three causes : The proper instruction of the soldiers at the commencement, the excellence of the quartermaster's department, and the admirable fitness of our commander, Colonel George Wright.

Our quartermaster was Captain (now General) Ralph W. Kirkham, and he fully satisfied all the requirements of his office. Never did a man more completely escape notice by the perfection of his work than did General Kirkham in the campaign of 1858.

The medical department was presided over by Surgeon J. F. Hammond, who stood high in his profession, but his temperament was impressionable to an uncommon degree. As a surgeon he had little to do—no bones to set nor wounds to dress. To show what false reports a man's senses may often make, I will relate in this connection an anecdote. One morning, towards the end of September, when I turned out there was a thick fog, and I was chilled and uncomfortable, and the air seemed to penetrate to the marrow of my bones. While I was feeling the worst, after starting, Surgeon Hammond joined me, his face radiant with unusual smiles, and he cried out: " Keyes, did you ever know such a glorious climate as this? It's perfect joy to live. I never felt so well in all my life." Then without waiting for a reply he galloped away out of my sight. I did not observe him again till near sunset, when we were in camp. In the meantime the atmosphere had undergone a complete change. The air was mild and smoky. I felt perfectly happy, and was forecasting the pleasures of San Francisco, when Hammond approached me again, beating his sides, his visage as gloomy as night. Coming near, he exclaimed: " Keyes, who ever knew such an accursed climate as this? Fire and thumping won't keep me warm. I've a mind to commit suicide." He did not wait to be consoled, but walked away, uttering maledictions against the weather.

Lieutenant John Mullan, of the Ninth Infantry, the

topographical engineer of the expedition, had in his former surveys made himself familiar with the country. In addition to his experience, he possessed uncommon mental and physical activity; he knew all the trails and fords, and in the crossing of streams which were not fordable his ingenuity was so remarkable that I dubbed him " Duke of Bridgewater."

It would be ungrateful in me to omit special notice of the company officers of my battalion. Ord, H. G. Gibson, Dandy, Flemming, Ransome, Morgan, and R. O. Tyler were conspicuous for their activity. Gibson (now General) was my subaltern lieutenant about eight years, and was always conscientious in the discharge of his duties. He was better posted in the laws and regulations of the army, and in the history of individual officers, than any man I have known. The readiness with which he could answer questions and cite authority saved me much labor, but tended to make me sluggish.

Lieutenant Lawrence Kip, Third Artillery, son of the Episcopal Bishop of California, performed his duty as my adjutant efficiently, and at the close of the campaign he wrote and published its history in a small book, which was reviewed in one of the English periodicals. On a re-perusal of Kip's work after finishing my own account, I find an exact correspondence of dates and few inaccuracies. The most that he said of Qualchein he borrowed from and credited to me.

The commander of our expedition, Colonel George Wright, a native of Vermont and a graduate of the Military Academy of the class of 1822, was every inch a soldier and a gentleman. In the year 1838 I heard Colonel Worth say of Wright, who was then a major, that he was entitled by his soldierly qualities to be advanced two grades. General Dandy, who was four times breveted for gallant conduct during the Rebellion, and who was my subaltern in 1858, considered Wright the best commanding officer he had served under. My position of second in command was one the difficulties of which have always been recognized by military men. The chief sometimes dislikes or envies his junior, and the latter fancies or discovers faults that he, if in command, would have avoided. From the commencement to the end of the campaign my relations with Colonel Wright were confidential and cordial, and if I were to give expression to my admiration and respect for that gallant soldier and gentleman, I fear my style would appear more flowery than the rules of rhetoric prescribe for a narrative of facts. The discipline he enforced was extremely rigid and severe. After crossing into the hostile country, reveille was at three o'clock A. M., and the hour of march generally five o'clock. One morning something delayed me, not above three minutes, but that was long enough to make it necessary for me to answer a brisk demand, through a staff officer, to explain why my column did not move at the time appointed. The rebuke was proper, although my delay was caused by no fault of my own, and at no time did I suspect for a moment that Colonel Wright would censure me unjustly or withhold praise that I deserved. Nothing in his conduct indicated that an acknowledgment of my deserts would dwarf his fame, and his order after the battle of the Spokan plains was profuse in the praise of the conduct of others, while it was silent in regard to his own. The passage in that order which related to me was in the following words:

"Captain E. D. Keyes, Third Artillery, commanding battalion, was energetic and gallant throughout. Although the troops extended over a mile, yet the captain was always in the right place in the right time."

I will relate a circumstance to show the estimate placed by the War Department upon the strength of the enemy opposed to Colonel Wright.

While at the Cœur d'Alene mission we learned that the Sixth Regiment of Infantry was on its way overland to Washington Territory. An order was addressed to Brigadier-General Albert Sidney Johnson, the same gentleman who, on the outbreak of the civil war, went South and was in command of the Confederate army at the battle of Shiloh, where he was killed. The following paragraph appeared in that order:

"If the commander in Utah should obtain information to cause him to believe it unsafe for the regiment to direct its march upon Walla Walla, he will order it by such other route as he may deem best."

It appears that General Johnson did receive information that caused him to apprehend danger to the regiment in the direction of Walla Walla, and he accordingly instructed its commander to proceed to Benicia, California, where in regard to expense and time of transport it was further from Walla Walla than at Salt Lake. For that reason I feared the Sixth Regiment would be detained in the harbor of San Francisco and I should be left in Oregon or Washington Territory.

In anticipation of such an arrangement, I addressed an application to General Clark to order me back to my old post, the Presidio. Colonel Wright endorsed my application as follows:

"The rank and long service of Captain Keyes, and particularly his zeal, perseverance, and gallantry during the present campaign, will, I trust, commend his application to the favorable consideration of the commander of the department.

"(Signed)   G. WRIGHT."

As soon as the report of Colonel Wright's operations and the result of the campaign were received at the head-

42

quarters of the army, then in New York City, Lieutenant-General Scott issued an order, dated November 10th, 1858, which was highly complimentary to General Clarke, commanding the Department of the Pacific, to Colonel Wright, and a large number of his subordinates, whose names are given. From John B. Floyd, who was then Secretary of War, no line or word of praise or satisfaction was received. Instead of acknowledging the merits of Clarke and Wright and breveting them, as they deserved, his treatment of both those officers was contemptuous. He reduced the command of the former by cutting off the northern portion, which embraced Oregon and Washington Territories, and erecting it into a new department, to the command of which he assigned the celebrated Brevet Major-General William S. Harney, who arrived at Fort Vancouver on the 24th day of October, 1858. I had a few days prior to that date arrived at the same post, with orders to proceed with my company to San Francisco.

I lost no time in paying my respects to the new commander, whom I had not seen before. He received me with ordinary politeness—in other words, he was not rude to me, though he was sufficiently taciturn. I had heard a great deal of General Harney, and of his extraordinary physical accomplishments and his prowess as an Indian fighter. I saw before me a man six feet two or three inches in height, faultless in proportion, complexion bordering on the sandy, head small, eyes and countenance ordinary. I felt at once that I was in the presence of a typical Southerner, and the coldness of his salutation inclined me to credit the reports or accusations I had heard that his official conduct towards Northern officers was often harsh. Captain Pleasonton, assistant adjutant-general, was present with his chief, and I asked him if there was any military news. The general interposed abruptly, saying: " None of the troops are to leave for San Francisco. I suppose that is what you want to know ? " I answered, " Yes, sir," without betraying any sort of emotion, although this hasty announcement of his decision was most unwelcome to me. I had heard that it was Harney's intention to renew the campaign against the Indians that Wright had so completely crushed, and the general reiterated that intention during my first interview with him. I considered his remarks as disparaging to all the officers engaged in the recent expedition, and especially to its commander. The Harney clique spoke inderision of our battles, in which not a man was hit, and their prejudices inclined them to withhold *all credit* from Wright and his associates, a great majority of whom were Northern men.

On going out from General Harney's office I met Surgeon Barnes, who was afterwards surgeon-general of the army, and one of the attending surgeons of President Garfield. He invited me to mess with him, and I gladly accepted his invitation, and took my meals with him while I remained at the post.

At that period Barnes possessed a sound body and a genial disposition; at the same time he was quite studious and methodical in his habits. He was so full of anecdotes of distinguished persons, and so generally fertile in discourse that I began to reconcile myself to the discomforts of Fort Vancouver, when on the morning of November 24 the steamer *Cortez* arrived from San Francisco, bringing news of the death of Colonel Frank Taylor and my consequent promotion to be major of the First Regiment of Artillery. Being no longer a company officer, General Harney gave me an order to repair to San Francisco and there await the official announcement of my promotion. The order was obliging to me, and it greatly modified my unfavorable impression of General Harney in regard to myself, but considering him as a prominent member of the sectional party to which I was so strongly opposed, I would not relinquish my vicarious resentment, which I cherished as a sacred duty.

COLOPHON

The Erasmus Keyes material on fighting Indians in the 1850s in Washington Territory was extracted from the 509-page edition of Fifty Years Observation of Men and Events *printed in New York City in that year by Charles Scribner's Sons. Most of this book is Civil War material, but General Keyes, formerly Captain Keyes, commanding the Third Artillery under Colonel George Wright, did serve in several Indian battles in Washington Territory. The 1884 book is held by a nmber of larger libraries but is moderately rare today. This booklet was printed in the workshop of Glen Adams, which is located in the sleepy country village of Fairfield, southern Spokane Couty in Washington State, and one township removed from the Idaho line. Typesetting of the title page was by Dale La Tendresse using a Compugraphic 7300 Editwriter computer photosetter. Camera-darkroom work for this edition was by Garry Adams using a Companica 660C camera and a LogE film processing machine. The sheets were printed by Trevor Del Medico using a 28-inch model KORS Heidelberg press. Folding, assembly and binding was by Garry Adams. This was a fun project. We had no special difficulty with the work.*